August 19, 1999

George –

We sincerely appreciate the opportunity to participate with BDPA.

We hope you enjoy this brief read.

Warmest Regards –

THE JOURNEY

THE JOURNEY

Revelations for Personal and Professional Relationships

By
Robert J. Selter
and
Gilbert J. Tumey

Elfin Cove Press
Seattle, Washington

ELFIN COVE PRESS
914 Virginia St.
Seattle, WA 98101

Cover design: C. Wilson Trull
Editing and page design: Laurel Strand

Library of Congress 98-072795

ISBN 0944958-44-3

Printed in the United States of America
1   3   5   7   9   10   8   6   4   2

Dedication

This book is dedicated to all of us
— human beings —
who, in our own unique ways,
face our private journeys to understand
and find happiness and meaning in life.

Acknowledgments

As with most writings, this book has been commented on and improved by a number of good friends. We sincerely appreciate their time and energy in assisting us on this project.

Our sincere thanks to Rachel Richardson, Darla Selter, Doug Taylor, and Shari Tumey.

A special thanks to Robert Spitzer, S.J., Ph.D., for his inspiration and friendship, and for being our partner in the synthesis of the material on which this book is based. We share his vision to take this awareness to all people for the betterment of the world.

Lastly, thanks to Finn Wolfe Contini for graciously allowing us to use his marvelous poem as the conclusion of this work.

We are humbled to know all of you.

Happiness cannot be pursued; it must ensue, and it only does so as the unintended side effect of one's personal dedication to a cause greater than oneself or as the by-product of one's surrender to a person other than oneself. Happiness must happen, and the same holds for success: you have to let it happen by not caring about it.

— Dr. Viktor E. Frankl

Inner Thoughts

It was a trip I dreaded taking.

My life was on a downhill slide. That month, I had to face some pretty ugly things. My mother had passed away in New York City at seventy-nine. She had been by herself. Although I was raised in and around New York City, I had lived on the West Coast for years. My only sister was in Florida.

My mother had held us all together after my dad died unexpectedly. I was fifteen. She went back to work and kept us going. She sacrificed to make do for the two of us kids, and to get us through college and launched in our independent lives. My sister and I kept in touch with her, though infrequently. Mother was a fine artist, with friends of her own in Greenwich Village, where she lived and worked.

None of us had much in common as adults. I always felt that my mother was struggling to find herself. She was extremely talented but, as I saw it, somewhat unfulfilled as an artist and a person.

Three weeks earlier, I had received a phone call from a relative telling me that my mother had passed away in a New York City hospital, alone and in pain. She died in a sterile white room among strangers waiting for her to expire so they could fill the bed with someone else. She never even told me she was ill. I should have been there! When she needed me the most, I was absent. No one to hold her, to help her through. I felt like a first-class slug.

On the work front, things were bleak, too. I was feeling the pressure of the company bureaucracy. From the time I was in college, I had told myself — no, I had promised myself — that I would never be caught in a job just to get the almighty buck. Yet here I was, an executive with all the perks — a huge corner office on the top floor of the company headquarters, mahogany furniture, executive assistant, big title. And, oh yes, having to watch my back at every turn so I didn't become expendable fuel for some egotistical peer's political aspirations to stardom and fame.

The politics were unbearable, and I was stressed beyond my limit — too much to do, too few people to do it, and off-the-chart expectations from senior executives to produce more in less time. Putting in twelve hours a day, six days a week. Sleeping two hours a night and worrying four . . . and inadequate results to show for it. I really had it all. All the perks meant zilch — just meaningless window dressing. What a nightmare.

Yeah, I really had it all! Who was I kidding? The pressure from work was seeping into every aspect of my existence. Not only was I not sleeping, I was starting to take out my frustrations on my family. I hadn't laughed or smiled in weeks. I was a highly compressed depression capsule waiting to explode. I knew it, and so did everyone around me.

So, I found myself on a plane from Los Angeles to New York, facing a week of doing double duty — presiding over a family gathering in honor of my mother (and trying to hide my guilt over not being with her), and looking good in a follow-up interview with an East Coast company pressing to hire me. Fleeing to the East Coast. My possible, but not realistic, escape. The prospect of uprooting my family and starting another career was frightening, to say the least. Just more to be depressed about.

The job I was interviewing for held some allure because it was new and different. But deep down, I knew it

The politics were unbearable. I was stressed beyond my limit, with off-the-chart expectations from senior executives to produce more with less.

would be just more of the same, with only a different view from the office window.

I couldn't remember ever feeling so vulnerable and off balance. A living hell, with no apparent way out.

Was this all I could expect from life? Financially, I was doing better than most. I was on track meeting the other career goals I had set for myself. Then why was I so miserable? There had to be more to life than this.

The Beginning

I settled into my aisle seat to brood through the non-stop flight to Kennedy International Airport. The center seat was empty, and the window seat was occupied by a kindly-looking, gray-headed fellow with a handlebar mustache, fifty-eight or so, several years my senior.

Through the plane's public-address system, we were politely told to secure our seat belts for take-off. As the flight attendant finished his safety message, my seatmate leaned toward me and said, "Hello, my name is Jake, Jake Jaspers." He was self-assured and calm — obviously secure with himself — and he smiled warmly as he addressed me.

And the journey began.

I was lost in my own anxieties about what was ahead of me in New York. I really wasn't interested in talking to a stranger. I mumbled, "Hi," hoping to convey that I didn't want to be bothered.

Neither of us said anything else until the plane leveled off at 31,000 feet. Jake seemed to sense my uneasiness and, as if to break the tension, made the usual airplane overture. "I'd guess, like me, you're going to New York," he said, smiling.

I nodded.

"What takes you there?" he asked.

And our conversation began.

At that moment, I had no idea that this six-hour flight and my conversation with Jake would launch me on an uplifting journey which would forever change the way I looked at myself and my life.

Engagement

As we shared our stories, Jake told me he lived in Portland, Oregon, but was going to visit his sister in New York for awhile. His father and brother were coming in from Quebec to join them at his sister's home for a brief family reunion. From there, he was traveling to Vermont on business. He was purposely arriving in New York a few days early so he could bum around and enjoy the city on his own.

As I listened to Jake, I couldn't help fidgeting. I was so uncomfortable with myself, I caught myself unconsciously raising my shoulders as if I were a tortoise trying to pull my head into my shell for protection from the world. I was hoping Jake would keep talking, so I wouldn't have to say anything. As I was thinking this, Jake stopped talking. "What about you?" he said.

Tersely, I laid out my current nightmare.

Jake gave a sigh of understanding. "I'm sorry to hear about your mother," he said. "That's a tough situation. But with you living on the West Coast, it seems almost impossible that you could have been there for her. Don't beat yourself up too badly about not being with her."

"Thanks," I said politely.

Jake shook his head from side to side and said, "What you're facing at work sounds all too familiar. It's got to be taking a heavy toll on you."

He was right. Was it so obvious?

Almost on cue, as though he had heard my innermost thoughts, Jake said matter-of-factly, "So, what *would* make you happy?"

"What? What did you say?" I blurted out.

Jake repeated his question.

"What do you mean, 'what would make me happy'?" I said, a bit annoyed that my feelings were so transparent.

Jake was not put off by my sarcasm. Instead, he smiled again, looked into my eyes, and softly said, "What would make you happy? I mean, starting right now, what do you really want for your life? What does happiness mean to you? Where do your passions lie? What do you want?"

I barely heard his last question. My mind was reeling with my deepest, most personal desires. I stared down the airplane aisle, not seeing anything, just lost in myself — *to be valued for my intelligence, my ideas, and my creativity; for my life to make a positive difference; to be appreciated, trusted, and respected.* I was alone in my dream, but I think I might have started to smile.

Distantly, I heard Jake's voice. His words startled me.

"If you understand yourself as a human being, and why you act the way you do, you can have it all."

If you understand yourself as a human being, and why you act the way you do, you can have it all. You can have the kind of life you really want to live.

New Awareness

Jake pulled down the center seat tray table, leaned on it facing me, and said, "Have you thought about exactly what makes you happy? What kind of happiness you are seeking *in your life*?"

I shook my head. "I guess I haven't really thought much about it," I said.

"Plato, the Greek philosopher, defined four kinds of happiness," Jake said. "In English, happiness is happiness. As Plato described it, though, there is a lot more discrimination and meaning for this one word."

He hesitated, leaned even closer, and began to whisper, as if he were about to confide in me one of his most cherished secrets. The sparkle in his eye was infectious. I leaned forward, too, ready to listen.

Focus

"The four kinds of happiness range from the least to the greatest sense of self-awareness," he explained. "They parallel the psychological view of human growth and maturity.

What kind of happiness are you seeking in your life?

"The first is immediate gratification. It focuses on stimulus/response reaction — the desire for food, for example. This form of happiness is immediate, intense, and concrete. It is gratification from the tangible. That hot fudge sundae!"

Jake licked his lips, acting out his pleasure in the thought. Then he added, "Of course, once it's consumed, it's gone. And the happiness it elicits is gone also. This is a really short-lived form of happiness.

"From the time each of us is born, we have these needs," he said. "And as long as this 'happiness' is kept in balance, we do okay. The trouble starts when this basic type of happiness overtakes our lives and becomes addictive. In some circumstances, it can consume all our attention and become overpowering. The happiness from immediate gratification then can become destructive. At this point, we become obsessed with the physical and the tangible, as happens with alcoholism and drug addiction.

"The second kind of happiness comes from personal achievement. In the life cycle, it is the development of our egos in adolescence. This happiness points inward. In its positive aspects, it creates the sense and desire in each of us to achieve. It's what stimulates competitiveness and creativity and, in our achieving, gives us self-esteem. But, like immediate gratification, if it becomes the source of our self-worth, the only meaning in our lives, it too can be personally destructive."

I raised my eyebrows and nodded. This was part of my problem at work — dealing with inflated egos and overly competitive peers. It had turned me and my co-workers into a bunch of jerks! Everyone was trying to control everyone else. And, of course, all of us acting that way — win at any cost — just put every one of us on the defensive.

As I thought this, I started to wonder what my part had been in creating this situation. How egotistical was I being? Was I threatened by others' contributions, and was I showing it? Was I afraid that others would look better than I would? Were my peers just reacting to my insecurities about working with them? Were they mirroring my behavior and showing their own insecurities about working with me?

Whatever the answers, it was obvious that in this environment, it was impossible to expect people to work as a team and to achieve good results through a common focus. That last meeting before I left. . . .

Jake said, "Hey, are you with me here?"

Laughing sheepishly, I said, "Yeah, keep going."

This was really starting to make sense. And I was beginning to think about my own actions.

"The third kind of happiness," Jake said, "is focusing to do good beyond oneself. This is also one of the stages that is often linked to maturing beyond self-centered ego as life's primary driver. Having one's ego in balance and feeling secure with one's self allows us to use our self-esteem and focus our energy on helping others. We can derive great pleasure from contributing and giving of ourselves. This is a natural human state. The vast majority of people are happiest when they're doing something good for its own sake, not to get something in return, and not for some personal ulterior motive or advantage. Sometimes this means simply being there for someone else, just listening and being supportive. Our presence for others — being there — carries a warm glow that literally touches other people. And the effect on us is that we are happy from merely giving.

"Ever since I can remember," he said, "both of my folks have quietly done things for others in our neighborhood. They've always been involved for other people.

Where each of us chooses to find our happiness controls everything we do. It controls all our relationships. It defines who we are. It dictates the meaning and purpose we seek in our lives.

Giving of themselves to others has always seemed to provide them inner peace. My dad used to tell us kids that the only things worth giving away are those you most want to keep for yourself. Now that's the true essence of giving!

"In my folks' case, this has been the giving of their time and energy. We never had much money, but if we had, I'm sure they would have found a good way to share that, too.

"Seeking the ultimate good is the fourth kind of happiness," Jake continued. "Plato explained this as not only doing good beyond oneself and for its own sake, but going to the next higher plateau, transcending to the ultimate — seeking ultimate love, beauty, justice, truth, and being.

"By nature, we human beings are 'ultimatizers,' but the spin we put on it is that we want it all, in the right order, with total clarity, all the time, when we want it!"

Jake and I laughed.

"The caution here," Jake said, "is that we not expect or demand 'the ultimate' from ourselves or from other people. It will only lead to unnecessary disappointment, frustration, and anxiety.

"So, where each of us chooses to find our happiness controls everything we do. It controls all our relationships. It defines who we are. It dictates the meaning and purpose we seek in our lives.

"Are we okay, so far?" Jake asked.

"I'm with you," I replied.

"Now, let me go back and make the link between these kinds of happiness," he said.

Crises with Change

"As we move through life and progress from one kind of happiness to the next higher one, we hit a wall — we go through an identity crisis concerning who we are and what we want out of life. This is the natural internal conflict that comes with maturing," Jake said.

"Let's start at the beginning, in early childhood.

"At about eight years old, children become unsettled about having their happiness fulfilled through physical things. They start to wonder if there is more to life than just food and warmth and satisfying the basic needs. They begin to say, 'I'm bored with this identity. I need more.' What emerges from their subconscious is an increasing awareness of their surroundings — things bigger than themselves. They realize they must grow up. They become anxious, knowing they cannot continue to derive their identity from their parents — from being their parents' kids or having their parents' friends as their own. They want their independence.

"The problem is," Jake continued, "children at this stage know they are separate from their parents, but they are only beginning to form their own identities. Children know who they *are not*, but not yet who they *are*; they have a negative identity. This creates conflict. Wanting to be 'my own self' but not knowing what that is creates anxiety and frustration. This shows up as moodiness in the pre-teen and early teen years.

"There are only three options to resolve this identity crisis." Jake held up three fingers, pointing to each as he spoke. "Comparing oneself to others, contributing beyond oneself, or seeking ultimate good.

"What's revealing is that roughly seventy per cent of adolescents experiencing an identity crisis turn to comparison as their path to defining who they are," he said.

"Do you know why?" he asked.

"No, why?" I said.

"Because they find stability and security in self-reliance. It's natural. Being 'better than others' and succeeding 'in comparison to' are tangible. They provide clarity and personal control," he said.

"Personally achieving and 'being better than' and 'having more than' are promoted in our culture. Our advertising emphasizes this. 'Are you a winner? Do you measure up?' These all imply that you'd better not fail or else you'll be a loser. And nobody wants to be a loser! So the inference here is not only achieving. It's doing so in comparison to others. It's competing. It subtly reinforces that success is only achieved by being over and against someone else. If competing is kept in perspective, it can be healthy. We run into problems, however, when we vest our whole self-worth in winning."

As Jake spoke, I saw how I had been driven deeper into this crisis in the last year or so. It was a matter of professional survival. Produce and succeed, or perish. It was me against my peers. It was even me against my own subordinates. It was the pressure of "I need to do this" and "I need to be that." Even though we were all supposed to work together, no one could stop looking out for "number one" long enough to function as a team.

Again, I had to ask myself what part of the "disconnect" at work was caused by my own actions? I had been so ready to blame everyone else! Maybe I played a large part in these failures.

I was getting lost in my own thoughts again. Jake's voice came back into focus as I reflected on this. He was saying, "The problem with the comparison game is that it's 'win, lose, or draw.' And if we *really* look into it, it's all 'lose.' The only focus is on 'me' — 'I,' above, over, and against everybody else. It's 'I must win at all costs.' And there is no 'I' in team. There is no 'I' in 'we.' "

I was beginning to realize that we were talking about me. I tried to be objective, but I was ready to hear more about myself.

Win, Lose, Draw

"On the surface, it may appear that 'winning' is a good deal. But that's the furthest thing from the truth," Jake said. "The 'win, lose, draw' game pits the 'winner' against everyone else, the 'losers.' So, if you are going to win, someone else has to lose. Since a winner can't stand to lose, let's look at losing first.

We were all supposed to work together, but no one could stop looking out for "number one" long enough to function as a team.

"If one is compelled to win, that is, if one is obsessed with winning, it is the *only* thing that matters. The mere possibility of losing is frightening. If you create a 'win' paradigm for yourself, and you lose, your self-talk will be terrible. You will find every reason to tell yourself that you are worthless. You'll hear yourself saying things such as: 'How could you be worth anything? In comparison to Milt, you got a smaller bonus than he did.' 'Jill got that bigger office when it became available. You didn't. You good-for-nothing!' 'Bob was asked by the boss for his advice, you weren't. What's wrong with you?' 'You are a loser. It is obvious. Everything points to it!'

"If you obsess enough this way, you will convince yourself that you have no self-worth. Before long, you will become jealous of those around you whom you perceive as winning more than you. You will get angry, not only with them for winning, but with yourself for losing. You will start to feel inferior. Since you think you're losing, you'll imagine that other people see you as a loser. *You loser!* Your own created inferiority complex will be inevitable, and it will jump up and smack you in the face.

"So, losing isn't the answer, is it?" Jake asked.

Jake's description was so depressing that I couldn't utter a word. I just stared at him.

He continued, "And, of course, any kind of pleasantry toward others, let alone trusting relationships with people, is out of the question.

"On the flip side, winning isn't much better," he said. "If you start to win, it will feed your ego, and you'll have to win more and more. Your desire for more 'success' will grow quickly, and getting what you just got won't satisfy you for long. To stay satisfied, you'll need to get more each time — more money, a better car, a larger office, the newest cellular phone, the newest status pen set. As long as your sole source of happiness is comparing yourself to others and winning, you'll need more and better.

"As a winner, you will also have trouble tolerating anything that you perceive as failure. In your compulsion, you will completely blow out of proportion any tiny little error you make. You will beat yourself up over even the slightest mistake, and you will be unable to tolerate even the smallest embarrassment. In a word, you will be miserable. But that's not all.

"This will lead to emptiness. You will begin to dislike everyone around you, and you'll let them know it. After all, they're not as good as you are. And if you're winning, they must be losing, right? You will feel contempt for them, and you will show your disdain. Of course, no one will want to be around you. The culmination will be your isolation from other people. You will be alone and resentful of everyone." Jake sat for a moment in silence.

I couldn't believe what Jake was describing. I was getting agitated, and at first I didn't know why. I shot back at Jake like a rifle bullet. I couldn't help myself.

Harshly, I said, "Gee, Jake, are you serious? Do you think people actually get that compulsive and go so far off the deep end?" I was hearing myself get very edgy. I knew what was wrong. We were talking about me, again. And it was too close to home.

Without hesitating, Jake answered me. "I've seen it," he said. "I've actually been there, and it's painful."

Jake took my anger in stride. I think he knew my outburst wasn't really directed at him, because he spoke softly back to me.

"Let's not go too far with this," he said. "For most people, this probably is an exaggeration. The point is, if you are conscious of what compulsive competition and 'winning at all costs' can do, you have the capability to check it before it gets so out-of-control. Remember, it isn't winning that gets you. It's when winning is the only thing that matters. It's the compulsion that traps you."

"I think I see that," I said, more calmly.

From Jake's expression, I think he knew he had hit a nerve. I was a little embarrassed, but said nothing more.

Jake went on.

"When you are obsessing, 'draw' isn't much of an option, either," he said. "It's nothing more than living in limbo, in the tense, anxious state of anticipating failure and losing.

"People stuck in the comparison game fluctuate back and forth among the win, lose, and draw scenarios — sometimes dozens of times a day. No matter which one you choose, it will be self-destructive. There is no way to win in the comparison game. No matter what the outcome, you lose," Jake concluded.

Jake must have seen the frown that formed on my face as he was talking. I felt tense and uncomfortable with the images his descriptions produced, because I knew some of this all too well for myself.

In an effort to recover my composure, I said as lightheartedly as I could, "I'm afraid I've bought these fortune cookies before, Jake, and it's a miserable existence."

It dawned on me that I had gotten to this painful point all by myself, without even knowing it. But I wasn't an overly competitive person. How could this happen to me?

I said, "You know, Jake, I don't think you have to be overly competitive to get sucked into the win-lose-draw game."

I paused for a second, thinking. "I can see that the need to survive at work has pulled me into that vicious cycle," I said.

"What do you mean?" Jake said.

"Well, I've always considered myself a team player. I don't think I often put 'me first' in my relationships. But lately, there's been so much pressure at work to produce, that I have felt — more than anything else — that I have to survive. What I'm starting to see, from what you've been talking about, is that the survival instinct is subconsciously pitting me against everyone else."

Jake nodded as I kept talking.

"If I'm feeling that I must survive, at all costs, it means I have to put myself first."

*Once you admit to yourself that you are in that vicious cycle of competition, you can do something about it. The way out is choosing to act **for** other people.*

I looked away from Jake and gazed into space, seeing nothing, but hearing myself say, "So, other people see me as wanting to compete with them, and they don't understand it. And their natural reaction is to defend against me by looking out for themselves first."

I turned back to look at Jake with a newfound understanding of what had happened to me at work. I said, "*I have created the competition by trying to survive the political pressure, and I've forced the people I want and need to team with to do the same.* Holy smokes! I'm beginning to see how this competitiveness operates against us.

"The last meeting before I left for this trip felt so strange to me," I said. "It was a meeting with some of my subordinates and some of my peers and their people.

"As others talked, all I could think about was how I was going to rebut their views. I was totally defensive and couldn't accept that what they were saying had value. All I could concentrate on was what I was going to say next just to keep the focus on me. I needed to be in control. I had to be the last one to speak, as though that would make me right!"

Jake said, "Competing can show up in subtle ways, but people are very perceptive. They know when you're being competitive. They may not understand it, but they can feel the tension."

"Yes, exactly," I said. "People ran out of that meeting and away from me like I had the plague."

"You know," Jake said, "our business environments have been built on competition. It is so prevalent that it's second nature. We don't even think about it. It's part of the daily work routine. We automatically react at work by competing with each other — and that kills our ability to cooperate.

"But it doesn't have to be that way. Once you see and admit to yourself that you are in that vicious cycle of competition, you can do something about it. The way out is choosing to act *for* other people, not competing against them. It's a lot less stressful to focus on a common goal with others and aim your energy to do good for something or someone else, instead of being guarded and protecting your own position. And it's a lot more fun. The way out is choosing to pursue 'doing good beyond yourself' as your primary motivation. This truly is when we are the happiest."

Real Life:
Getting to a Higher Viewpoint

"We really do have a choice, you see," Jake said. He stared at me with an intensity that seemed to rivet us eye-to-eye and mind-to-mind. I found it impossible to look away from him.

"We can choose to operate from an egotistical, self-promoting, 'all-for-me-and-to-hell-with-you' position. We can be over and against others, looking for the bad news about them, treating others as objects and using them for our own advantage. In other words, we can view people as problems.

"And what do we typically do with problems? We 'dispense' with them. We *fix* them. They are 'things' to be dealt with. So that's what we do! Or, as you described about your last meeting, we avoid people who cause problems. That's what people did to you. They got away from you as soon as they could."

For the first time since Jake began talking, I could see sadness on his face and hear agitation in his voice. He must have just flashed on an unpleasant experience of his own.

"I was a very successful businessman for a long time," Jake said. "Over several years, I had built a company from the ground up until it became very successful." Jake looked down at his lap and, in a shaky voice, added, "At least, it was financially successful. But it never came close to its real potential."

He looked up and continued. "I had started this company with two good friends, with whom I shared a common vision. We stuck together for a long time and made it work. Boy, it was exciting!"

Jake smiled as he reminisced. "Three guys freely sharing and exploring together without any regard for who said what or who was 'on top.' We didn't care who got the credit for what. Hell, we didn't even think about getting credit. None of us cared at all about that."

As he spoke, Jake got more and more animated.

"The three of us were on top of the world. We were doing exactly what we wanted to do, without any bureaucracy to suffocate us. Without any politics to contend with. It was pure fun! The icing on the cake was that we were making real money doing it."

Jake's excitement waned as he described what happened next. He continued almost in a whisper, with what I interpreted as guilt in his voice.

"It all came crashing down, though, in our last year of business. Actually, 'it' didn't come crashing down. The truth be known, I made it happen," he said.

"I don't know when it started, or even how it happened, but unconsciously, I lost sight of who I was. I started to turn the business into a 'me only' proposition. I found myself using my two friends for my personal advantage, to make me look good — as if I was the only one responsible for our success.

"Before long, the three of us had some knock-down, drag-out arguments. The upshot was that the other two guys decided to move on together without me. I was left with a fair amount of money, but not much else.

"I was really bitter for several months," he said. "I was empty. I went into a tailspin. I started drinking heavily, and became more and more disconnected from my family and all the other things I loved."

Jake stared straight ahead, as though I wasn't there. It was as if he was having a private conversation with himself. "I created my own win/lose crisis. I had made competitiveness my primary focus, and I didn't see that until it was too late. For a long time, I blamed everyone else for what happened. I especially blamed my two friends. But all the while, I knew deep down that I had created this mess for myself.

"I was in terrible pain. I hated myself. But at least I still had enough sense to ask for help. I called my father. My dad and I talked once in a while, just to catch up on each other's lives. He is a retired psychologist and had spent the last few years traveling. Along with studying psychology and its historical roots, he's always been a buff on the ancient European and Asian philosophers. When I called him, I started with the usual small talk. We chitchatted for a while, until he finally said, 'Son, what's wrong. You sound troubled.' Well, that did it."

Jake looked away and laughed to himself. He turned back to me with a small smile and said, "I bawled like a baby." He kept chuckling as he spoke. "Can you picture that? Me, a grown man, a successful businessman crying into the phone to his father like a nine-year-old kid."

He grew serious again. "Actually, that cry was the be-ginning of my re-entry into humanity. After about a minute of non-stop sobbing — which seemed like an hour to me at the time — I was able to tell my dad what was going on. We decided I should come see him at his cabin in Maine to talk and get re-connected. So, I did.

"During the day, we took long walks around the lake his cabin is on, and we talked. In the evenings, we sat in front of his stone fireplace and talked more. We talked about everything. My childhood, my mother's illness and passing, my brother and sister, and, of course, where I was with myself in my life.

"It was the best therapy in the world. What you and I have been talking about is a mix of my own experiences and what I learned from my dad.

"After that time in Maine, I finally got around to being honest with myself. When I did, I felt embarrassed and humiliated. But after a while, once I admitted that I was the problem, things started to change.

"What actually changed," Jake said, "were my own attitudes. I was able to view things from a different perspective. When I stopped blaming others, I could see things more clearly. And by being honest, but not judgmental, I was able to see my own role in what happened. I gained a higher viewpoint of my actions and my life.

"The more I talked to myself, the worse I felt about what I had done. But I also felt uplifted and free to act on my new knowledge."

Jake paused to take a breath. Hanging on his every word, I said, "What did you do?"

"The first thing I did was to refocus beyond my own self-pity, and get my attitude back on track — concentrating on the contributions I could make with my talents. This took a few months, I'll tell you."

"What did you do?" I interrupted.

Jake laughed and said, "Didn't you just ask me that?"

We laughed together. He kept going.

"I stopped blaming everyone else for my problems and started to think about the good things in my life. After first working on my relationships at home with my family, I turned to re-establishing a relationship with my business partners."

"Wasn't that difficult to do?" I asked.

"Well, you'd think so," Jake said. "But actually, it wasn't. After the hell I went through realizing how competitive I had been, I was so focused on making things right that I was able to face my two friends honestly and openly, although I was a bit anxious about their reaction at seeing me and hearing what I had to say."

"How did it go?" I asked.

"I called them and made an appointment to visit at

their office," Jake said. "I couldn't believe how open these guys were, and how glad they were to see me. When they came to the door to let me in, none of us said a word. We just hugged each other for what seemed a long time."

Jake beamed.

"When we sat down, I spoke first. I just laid it out and apologized for how I'd acted. I told them the hell I'd been through since we split up.

"They tried to keep the conversation light, downplaying what I had done. I told them I appreciated their attitudes, but that I had amends to make with them.

"I told my two former partners that I had a proposal for them. I told them that I knew they had done very well since we parted ways, and of course from our prior business, they knew I had done okay as well. So, my offer was, I guess, even more dramatic, since money was not my focus.

"I told them that I wanted to re-engage with them. To offer my services to them and their business in whatever way I could help. For a year. For nothing."

I was spellbound.

"I told them my motivation was to re-establish our

mutual trust, and that I was committed to contribute with and for them."

"What did they say?" I asked.

"They were as stunned as you look now," Jake said.

We both laughed again.

"We talked for several hours about what happened, and why I did what I did," Jake said. "They mentioned several times how they had wanted to contact me and see how I was doing, but didn't because they weren't sure how I would react. We all repeatedly said how much we missed each other and missed the energy and feelings we had in the old days when we had started together.

"To make a long story short, my partners accepted my offer, in part. The part they refused to accept was my working for free. Although I was totally sincere about that, they wouldn't hear of it. The agreement we struck was that I would re-join them as a partner in their firm, and that we would continue from there.

"We've been working now for six months, and it's more and more like old times, with the renewed shared vision we had early on. So, things are working out.

"What I've been experiencing," Jake said," is that when I choose to operate from an attitude of selflessness, from the higher view of what I can contribute, without first seeking benefit for myself, my view of the world changes. As a result, how I act with others changes, too. My relationships are more positive.

"I take the focus on 'me' out of the relationship equation. By doing this, I unconsciously focus on doing the right things for the right reasons. And the irony is, I never have to worry about myself. Good things seem to happen naturally.

"The other thing that happens is when I'm not focused on getting things for myself, I wind up getting more credit for the things I do.

"You know, it's amazing that we can choose how we want to be. I mean, we can look at life and all we do from the perspective of wanting to help others. We can choose to contribute and to support people. We can choose to treat people with respect. We can choose to be proactive listeners — really listening and valuing other people's views before we focus on our own, joining in common cause with them and looking to do a good for someone or something else beyond ourselves.

"The real magic is that when I act from that *higher viewpoint*, I tend to have a positive effect on people I

When I choose to oper-
ate from an attitude of
selflessness, from the
higher view of what
I can contribute, my
view of the world
changes. How I act
with others changes,
too. My relationships
are more positive.

deal with. Even when I don't affect those who are obviously trying to compete with me, I see what they are doing, and their competitiveness doesn't rub off on me.

"Existing to compete, to be better than, produces anxieties within ourselves and destroys any hope for meaningful, trusting relationships," Jake said. "Just look at how I acted and what happened with my partners, or what happened in your last meeting just before this trip. Our focusing on 'me first' is always seen for what it is. People know instinctively when we are phony — not authentic. We don't fool anybody by appearing to act for someone else's benefit or for a team goal, then turning around and acting in our own interest. The old saying 'actions speak louder than words' is really true. People are smart. They know what's going on.

"There is another subtlety about the anxiety that competing produces," Jake said. "It's not only mental stress. It's also physical. We always talk about being 'uptight.' Well, that's what the anxiety produces. It literally tenses all our muscles and constricts our capillaries. It prevents open flow of blood to our brains. We truly cannot think clearly with all our faculties."

Jake shrugged. "How can we be creative and open to

others' ideas when we are tense? How can we put the thoughts and feelings of others first when we're like this?"

No response from me was necessary.

Jake concluded with a statement that I have kept close to me ever since. In a matter-of-fact tone, he said, "So, if we choose to, we really do create our own reality."

Jake paused. We both diverted our attention to the flight attendant. He was coming down the aisle pushing a beverage cart. I glanced at my watch and was surprised to discover how fast this flight was going.

Then Jake started up again, relating the idea of a higher viewpoint from another angle.

Magnified Effect

"This higher viewpoint also applies to organizations," Jake said. "When we first sat down, you were telling me how difficult things are at work, how competitive you and your peers are.

"When a company's focus to be successful shows up internally as competition among its own people, it can spell failure for everyone involved.

"Company strategies and goals for success can all too easily get translated into 'get the money' and 'kill the competition.' This sets employees up to compete with one another in the urgency to beat the competition. It can seep inside the organization and become a warrior's chant of destruction. As the pressure to produce increases, the 'kill or be killed' mentality can quickly become each person's focus for survival."

I winced. Jake's scenario fit so well with my own need to survive at work.

"Those words may seem brutal in connection with business," Jake continued, "but the underlying tone of what I described can become the model people adopt. That's why competitions arise among internal players. That's why attempts at team-building tend to be short-lived. Nobody trusts anybody else. The smiles and cordial comments around the office become insincere and false. And everyone in this compulsive game feels the tension."

"I see what you mean," I interjected. "It's difficult to focus on trusting each other and working as a team when the atmosphere in the air is warlike."

"You're right," Jake said. "The pressure put on employees to 'beat the competition' sets the stage for a vicious, downward, no-win spiral. If executive management really pushes it, not only will the internal competition reach a fever pitch, but the ethical basis of how business is done can also start to erode. If the goal is to beat the competition *at all costs*, then cheating, lying, and stealing become justified under the crusade of what's good for the company.

"Once this starts, it's hard to stop. And the longer it continues, the worse it gets. If it's not recognized and checked, the internal competition will reach into every department. Then it will spread within them. The company will do worse and worse. Eventually, it will find itself in a major downward plunge until it is competing for its very survival.

"There is a way out, but it takes the commitment to do things differently," Jake said. "Everyone needs to take a deep breath, relax a little, and look at the situation from the higher viewpoint we've been talking about. The focus needs to be on what will really make people happy, what people really want."

"That's powerful! But how would you go about making it happen?" I asked.

"Open and honest discussions need to take place —

about everyone's need to feel that what they do and how they contribute makes a difference. That their lives matter. That their efforts positively affect the company," Jake said. "Then, actions need to be taken to change the atmosphere in the company so people genuinely feel these beliefs as the norm. It will require a different mindset by the company leaders. They must commit to and model their belief in the dignity and respect for every person as a unique human being.

"It may surprise you, but higher pay isn't the answer," Jake said. "We would all like to bring home a bigger paycheck. But numerous studies show that most people leave their employers because they're not treated with respect and dignity. It's not the money.

"They leave because they have no say in the decisions or the processes that affect them and what they do at work. They don't feel valued, and they don't believe that their talents and energy and passion are viewed as making a difference. They typically leave, or escape I should say, because they are not appreciated and not allowed to be creative. They resent being micro-managed and openly push back from it.

"They leave because they have no opportunities for

education to fulfill their desire to learn, and because they are not treated as thinking, feeling, caring human beings. Inadequate pay typically comes in seventh or eighth out of ten reasons why people leave," Jake said.

"The reason money gets so much emphasis is because when people are not afforded the dignity and respect they believe they deserve, the way they get back is to demand more money. It comes from feeling trapped and not in control of the situation. In other words, if you are not going to give me the respect I want, then I'll make you pay to get me to stay here!

"A sad state of affairs, don't you think?" Jake asked.

"Yes, it is," I replied. "It makes sense, though."

Jake continued. "I honestly don't think people are unreasonable. But when they feel manipulated and constrained, they can get compulsive.

"You know, what a lot of people tend to do is to blame all this on 'the bosses.' But I think the reality is that 'the bosses' are also stuck with how they grew up in business, and what they learned about how to be successful, just like the rest of us. I don't think they intentionally mean to ignore people's wants and needs.

"Don't you think the executives you work for feel

pressure and sometimes feel trapped and out of control? Don't you think they would like to be appreciated and thanked for the work they do, for the time they put in and for the tough decisions they make all the time? You bet they would!

"For the most part, their situation is no different from yours. They're just playing at a different level with a different definition of their identity. But it's the same game," Jake said.

"And you know why this is all true?" he asked.

I thought for a second. "Well, at least around me, the executives I work with always seem to be on top of everything. But I guess they question themselves privately, too," I said.

"I think that's true," Jake said. "They're human beings with the same wants that you and I have. It's the one thing we all have in common. If we were to treat each other the way we would like to be treated, we would do fairly well. So, let's get back to making it happen.

"With input from all levels, management needs to sit down and talk about changing the work environment to honor and dignify people. Change the culture.

Management needs to model this behavior and take the steps that signal to everyone that all employees are respected and trusted.

"Over time, things will change. Trust among people will develop. Dignity and respect for each other will become the norm. The excitement of people working with and for each other will make the place hum." Jake's eyes gleamed with excitement.

"The new trust will breed personal commitment and accountability to others. Work will become not only fun, but an exciting adventure shared by everyone in the company," he said.

"The result will be mutual loyalty and caring. One, *just one*, of the results will be a gigantic leap in quality. The traditional business benefits are almost a by-product of people feeling good about who they are and doing the good they can do for a common goal beyond themselves. People will make better business decisions, for the right reasons, including for the good they can do as people working together.

"In the long run, the companies that understand and embrace these principles will truly have the competitive edge. They will be the ones that survive," Jake predicted.

"The routine management meetings to discuss what to do about low morale ratings in the latest company-wide employee survey will be unnecessary. High morale will be normal.

"The environment must be made safe. People must be allowed to make mistakes without fear of punishment, and they must be involved in creating their own destinies. When these conditions exist, people become motivated to do the best they can as a team.

"Genuinely progressive companies recognize the power that arises when people feel good about themselves and their environment. They will take it to yet a higher level. They will invest in the well-being of employees' families, because they know this will make employees feel good and cared for. These companies will initiate programs that support families, such as on-site day care centers, recreation facilities, and so on.

"Most companies don't think about employees' families much, if at all," Jake said. "But employees' families are important to the company.

"Why do you think I say that?" he asked.

"I think it's simple," I said. "We are whole human beings. All of our experiences and fears and frustrations and good feelings are intertwined. If I am not happy at home, I'll be less likely to be happy or productive at work, and vice versa.

"I sure have felt that lately," I added. "My feelings about work have made me an ogre at home. And then I bring that rage back to work."

Jake nodded in agreement.

"Let me make this 'whole person' connection another way," he said. "If the company honors my entire existence by respecting my personal needs, gives me the flexibility to deal with my whole life during the day, and trusts me to produce and do my work, then I will feel dignified as a person. I will also feel the personal responsibility not to abuse this mutually trusting relationship. And what will happen? I'll treat others in the same way. They will see my desire to trust them and support them, as well. I mean other people in my own department and in the rest of the company, and the suppliers and customers I work with, too.

"See what I mean?" Jake asked.

"I sure do," I replied.

Jake went on. "At its foundation, business is a network of people. And people who treat each other with respect will enjoy being together and will enjoy being successful together.

"This also extends to the communities in which we live and where companies operate. The broadest definition of company success can go beyond profit, and even beyond support to employees. It can include the good the company can do in the community. The payback to the company is that the community will view it as a good neighbor and see that it is focused beyond itself for the greater good of others. Other organizations in the community with whom the company interacts, and from whom it may need assistance, will be more interested in the company's welfare and needs. Successful companies know this and are very involved in their communities.

"What I've seen is that companies may initially get involved in their communities because 'it is good for business,'" he said. "To do this, the company will enlist employees to support community activities in the company's name. Fairly quickly, these employees get hooked on the tremendous satisfaction they derive from giving. It becomes another 'people helping people' network in the company's name.

"All of this is doing good beyond self. It comes full

All of this is doing good beyond self. It comes full circle — at a personal and family level, at a team and departmental level, at a company level, and at a community level — for people. The greatest amount of good is achieved for the largest number of people.

circle — at an individual and personal level, at a family level, at a team level, at a departmental level, at a company level, and at a community level — for *people* — employees and their families, executives and managers, stockholders, suppliers, and customers and for the local and broader community. The greatest amount of good is achieved for the largest number of people."

Jake really had my attention. I caught myself raising a full glass of orange juice to my lips, wondering where the refill had come from.

Extraordinary Teaming

"I guarantee a much higher level of success if everyone involved decides to team with a common vision and makes commitments to each other," Jake continued. "This is true in business, in civic groups, in religious organizations, in neighborhoods, in families — in any and every human relationship.

"The commitments on which extraordinary relationships are built and which are necessary for outstanding teaming include every single person promising to: contribute, not compete; create internal win/win situations instead of win/lose problems; not complain about and blame others; give and show respect; and trust.

"These have nothing to do with pay or position or title or education or any of that," Jake said. "These are commitments made between human beings to each other. They are humble promises of the heart made on a person-to-person basis. They are real commitments that make a difference in doing real work."

Jake looked straight at me and said, " 'I promise that my intentions and actions are to contribute to our common goals and purpose together. Will you promise the same to me?'

" 'I promise to find ways for us all to win together. I will not consider win/lose positions. Will you commit the same to me?'

" 'I will focus on the good things you do and on your good intentions. Will you promise the same to me?'

" 'I promise to respect you for your ideas, your energy, your creativity, and all the good things I see about you. Will you promise the same to me?'

" 'I promise to trust you and to give you plenty of slack as we work together. Will you promise the same to me?'

"As we're sitting here talking, these commitments make sense, don't you think? Don't they seem like logical steps to good teaming?" Jake asked.

"Yes, of course," I said.

"These commitments really take root when I have to use them and I don't want to. When everything is rosy between us, it's not a big deal, is it?" Jake said. "The real test is when I disagree with you on an important issue. Things start to change when I don't want to trust you or respect your opinion, but I decide I will.

"The first time I am successful in keeping my commitments to you — for our mutually trusting relationship — I have turned the corner. Every successful test from then on just strengthens our respect for each other. And our relationship gets stronger and stronger. That is powerful medicine!" Jake exclaimed.

Jake was raising his voice in excitement. "Can you imagine the difference in the atmosphere if we shift today's normal unspoken work ethic of 'I will only trust you when you prove to me that you can be trusted' to that open, free, and magnificent paradigm of 'I start by respecting you as a human being and trusting you to the limit until you show me otherwise'?"

Imagine the difference in the atmosphere if we shift from today's unspoken work ethic of "I will only trust you when you prove to me you can be trusted" to that magnificent paradigm of "I respect you as a human being, and I will trust you to the limit."

He kept talking louder and louder. "Wow! The excitement we will generate! The energy we will have! The good things we will do! The pride in 'us' we will share!"

Suddenly, we realized that people were looking at us. Hunkering down in our seats, we looked at each other and giggled like little kids. It was great!

Then we fell silent. I was thinking about everything we had been discussing.

Safe Landing

The flight attendant's voice came over the public-address system. "We are beginning our descent into Kennedy International. Please make sure your seat belts are fastened and your tray tables are secured in their upright position in the seat ahead of you. We will be landing in just a few minutes."

Jake and I checked our seat belts. He reached up and latched the tray table between us.

Our flight was nearly over.

As the wheels touched down on the runway, I felt a surge of optimism that things were going to be different in my life. Things were going to work out. I no longer felt depressed. I felt inspired about what could be.

Jake was looking through the window, watching us land.

I said to him, "Listen, do you have any free time while you're in the city? Is there a chance we could get together while we're both still in town?"

"Why, yes," he replied. "I have a couple of days just to kick around before I meet with my family. I'd really enjoy seeing you again."

"Thanks, Jake," I said. "Then let's get together."

We met the next evening for an early dinner. We wound up sightseeing some of my favorite spots, but they held a new perspective for me. The ice-skating rink at Rockefeller Center seemed to be a fantasy oasis. The evening lights on the ice gave the place a warm, surrealistic glow in the midst of the dark and otherwise pressure-packed city surrounding it. I watched the skaters freely enjoying themselves and smiling and laughing with other skaters. Why couldn't relationships always be like this? Why do we think we need to "get away" to some special place to have fun? Don't we deserve to be happy all the time?

We visited the Empire State Building, viewing from

the observation deck as far as the eye could see, across the city and far beyond into the surrounding areas. This panoramic view took on new meaning. It made me ponder what horizons I wanted to imagine for myself. What I really wanted to do with my life. How far I could apply my talents and my energy for a more meaningful, fulfilling existence. It was a much different view than I would have had just a day earlier.

Our early evening dinner turned out to be an all-nighter at a coffeehouse not far from my hotel. We talked long into the night and finally parted ways after exchanging addresses and phone numbers with promises to keep in touch. Our parting handshake turned into an embrace of understanding and affection.

I made it through the family gathering for my mother better than I expected. Visiting with aunts, cousins, and friends of my mother who had known her after I left home, I realized that she was a fulfilled person after all. Through her friends' eyes, I saw her not merely as my mother, but as a whole person. I had not thought about her non-family interests. I had been unaware of the rest of her life. It was obvious she was loved by and had influenced many people besides my sister and me.

The panoramic view took on new meaning. It made me ponder what horizons I wanted to imagine for myself. What I really wanted to do with my life.

I went to the follow-up interview for that possible new job and decided the job was not at all what I wanted. I guess I had known that before, but finally admitted it to myself. Ironically, they kept calling me for several weeks after I returned to Los Angeles, sweetening their offer each time. But I knew that going with that company would have been too much of a compromise. It would not have made me happy.

Reflections

The flight home from New York was spent on introspection and reflection. I wound up in a window seat with an empty seat between me and the aisle. Being by myself gave me a chance to think about the previous week — especially the conversations with Jake.

As I thought about everything we had discussed and my situation at work, it became clear to me that things could change if I wanted them to, and if I was willing to do something about it on my own.

I decided that trying to make an opportunity to change my job was just an escapist idea. I enjoyed my job and my co-workers. I decided that the only way to change what happened at work and in my relationships was to change my own perspective and how I acted and reacted. What this boiled down to was how I chose to manage and focus myself, and how I chose to behave in my relationships with others.

I thought back to two things Jake had said a week earlier.

"If you understand yourself as a human being and why you act the way you do, you can be happy."

"If we choose to, we really do create our own reality."

It made sense that everything must start with me.

My own motivation — either to actively compete with others (or be drawn into competing from fear and the need to survive) or to go beyond myself in working with others for a common focus — is *the key*. My internal motivators will drive what I think and how I act. These, in turn, will shape my attitudes and express themselves as I deal with other people.

How well I relate to and manage myself will manifest itself in my relationships with others.

Everything that happens to me, then, is rooted in my relationship with myself.

How authentic do I want to be with myself? Do I keep

my commitments to myself? Am I honest with myself about how I feel and what I want, or do I lie to myself and play games?

Do I feel okay about who I am? If not, why not? And what am I willing to do about correcting whatever it is, so I am comfortable with who I am and how I act?

I began to see that I could only be honest and authentic with others if I am willing first to be that way with myself. In a way, it comes down to how much I respect\myself. If I can't respect myself, how can I respect anybody else? And if I don't respect others around me, won't they see it in the way I act toward them?

If I follow this full circle, it seems that people mirror back to me how I think of them and treat them — and it is all founded on how I feel about myself!

So, I ask myself — to what extent have I created my own hell at work (and everywhere else, for that matter)? I can't change what happens, but I can choose how I respond to events, and I can definitely choose how I want to act toward people!

I can choose my own attitudes. If I choose not to be protective and defensive and destructively competitive, it is very hard for others to be defensive toward me.

If we choose to, we really do create our own reality.

What freedom this is! To determine for myself to be outgoing and to be authentic with people — to express myself truthfully for who I am. To do things for the sake of doing them, to support others, and work toward a common goal. To *not* worry about myself or put myself first before thinking of others or our common goals.

As I say these things to myself, it affects how I feel. I feel peaceful thinking about extending beyond myself. It is exciting and refreshing!

But thinking of "me first" makes me feel anxious. It doesn't feel good.

It's strange. If I am comfortable with myself, I am not threatened by other people. This allows me to act and respond to others openly, trusting and respecting them.

I can disagree with someone and still convey caring and respect for that person. I do not define another's personal worth by his or her opinion on an issue. Because I am at peace with myself, focused to contribute, I can disagree and still show genuine respect. People will feel this respect and will reflect the same back to me.

This is humbling stuff!

So, I commit to being authentic with myself. I will

love myself, and I will take care of myself. This will allow me to do the same with others.

I choose to do the good that is beyond myself. Just the thought of this makes me happy.

It all begins with me.

Continuing the Journey

After a couple of days back on the job, thinking about my conversations with Jake, I decided not to let the job or the system intimidate me anymore. I decided I needed to manage what happens to me. I decided to focus on the good I can do beyond myself.

Now, I consciously check myself to make sure this is what motivates my desire to achieve. It is the idea of "doing the good" that I have chosen as the measure of who I am and what I am all about. This way, everything is kept in its proper balance.

With these insights, my relationships with people have improved. Along with my reflections and commitments to myself, the "higher viewpoint" Jake talked about on the plane is making a difference. I am more conscious of people's behavior. When I experience people acting competitively or compulsively, I recognize it more readily. This enables me to be more empathetic and not take their negative comments personally.

This squarely places the responsibility on how I get along with people on me, not them. It's true. How I get along with people is up to me. How I choose to act and react with them is totally my choice, not theirs. I find that I am really free to pursue the good that I can do and not get caught up in the "win/lose" competition game.

Of course, I still catch myself acting egotistically. When I do, I whisper to myself, "That's not really me." I think I am improving, though. More and more I automatically put others' interests before my own when I talk and act, instead of focusing first on what I want.

I am more aware of people around me who seem anxious and uptight. I wonder how happy and fulfilled they are. I wonder if they have settled for "I guess this is how it's supposed to be," as I had. I remember how I used to suffer through the indignities and drudgery of the workday, just trying to hold on until the end of the shift so I could go home and "live," but still knowing that I would take my frustrations and anger with me, no matter where I went.

I don't think this journey ever ends. You just keep focusing for the sake of the bigger picture, and to whom and what you can contribute that is bigger than your own needs.

I wonder how their lives could change if they could see they can create their own positive reality of what they want, and how freeing it can be — that under-living their lives is a choice they don't have to settle for. Then again, they didn't spend time with Jake.

I am finally free for myself and have taken the responsibility to be accountable for myself.

This new way of thinking has had another unexpected effect. Although I had thought about it once in a while, I never took the time to extend myself into the community. Now, I have started to look where I can be helpful and add value beyond my home life and work environment. I am looking for places where I can contribute and where I can best apply my talents and my time to be of service.

I don't think this journey ever ends. Once begun, you just keep focusing for the sake of the bigger picture, and to whom and what you can contribute that is bigger than your own needs.

This is what feels good. This is what makes me happy.

Tenderly We Tread

The sun rises over a barren landscape
What should be fertile grounds is not
First light casts no shadows
For nothing grows in this land

The seeds are in the soil
The soil is rich in nutrients
There is plenty of water
The conditions are right for growth

But nothing grows in this land . . . yet.

Perhaps what is needed is cooperation
An equal effort from all
Proper cloud cover to hide the sun awhile
And enough rain for the plants to grow

The first shoots will need tenderness
If there's a brutal wind it's back to square one
But the wind is pleasant
And instead carries the seeds of future generations

This story could be the human soul
So much potential . . .
Hate is harshness and harshness is barren
Love and understanding is bountiful

So there is hope for the landscape after all.

Finn Wolfe Contini
December 1997

About the Authors

Jed Selter and Gil Tumey are partners in the Institute for Personal and Professional Effectiveness (IPPE). They formed the Institute out of a passion to help people enrich their lives and improve their relationships.

Their vision is to help people positively affect their own lives and those of others by being inspired and fulfilled human beings.

Between them, Jed and Gil have more than sixty years of business experience, from line to executive management, spanning highly responsible positions in commercial and non-profit companies, as well as the U.S. military. Collectively, they have more than forty-two years of management experience with an internationally successful Fortune 50 company.

Throughout their careers, Jed and Gil have been innovators for forward thinking in the areas of personal and organizational effectiveness. Individually and together, they advocate progressive and responsible employee empowerment. They believe that respecting and dignifying people in the workplace as "whole persons" is essential to lasting business success. They are proponents of the philosophy that attracting, developing, and retaining the most competent workforce is a key factor for business success and depends on providing a work environment in which people can be inspired and fulfilled, both personally and professionally.

Jed and Gil have been guest and keynote speakers at forums and seminars on the topics of motivation, leadership, effective management, and team-building.

Unprecedented Team Results Through Inspired People

Can you imagine being a member of a group of people who are singularly focused for outrageously successful results? Who use their unbounded energy, creativity, and skills to produce the highest quality?
And, who support each other toward a common vision through mutual trust and respect?

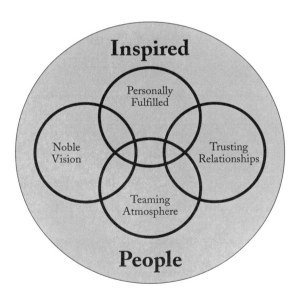

The partners of IPPE provide the learning, materials, tools, and tailored support to make this exciting proposition of success a reality for your organization, group, or team.

IPPE Focus

The Institute is dedicated to helping people and organizations improve their effectiveness to meet objectives. The Institute was founded out of a passionate drive to improve the lives of a broad spectrum of people — and in doing so, to provide the basis for exceptionally positive relationships. This is considered vital in these times of rapid change, increasing demands on people, mounting pressures to produce, and burn-out.

As a foundation for assimilation, IPPE draws on basic concepts of ethics and integrity to convey the principles of personal and professional effectiveness. IPPE teaches how to apply principles of trust and respect in creating and maintaining a dynamic organization in which people desire to freely contribute their full potential and goodwill.

Benefits

IPPE's work with people is highly relevant for both individuals and organizations:

- Intensified Personal Commitment
- Increased Creativity
- Happier, Energized People
- Improved Quality and Productivity
- Trusting Relationships
- Adaptability and Flexibility
- Enhanced Quality of Life
- Improved Decision-Making
- Effective Communication
- Reduced Turnover
- Synergistic Teams
- Broadened Organization Success

About IPPE

The partners have extensive experience in building and promoting common visions, responsible personal empowerment, trusting relationships, and effective teaming. IPPE can accelerate attainment of desired results through inspiring people to want to contribute.

If we can be of assistance to you or your organization, please contact The Institute for Personal and Professional Effectiveness or MountainTop Experience, our partner in Johannesburg, South Africa.

The Institute for Personal & Professional Effectiveness

704 228th NE, Suite 843

Redmond, WA 98053

Phone: (425) 702-4727

Toll-free: 1-888-334-2911

E-mail: ippe@ippe.com

MountainTop Experience

PostNet Suite 141

Private Bag 9

Melville 2109

South Africa

Phone: 27-11-462-3716

E-mail: cbt@gem.co.za

Fax: 27-11-482-5419

Order Form

Additional copies of *The Journey* may be ordered by mail, fax, or e-mail.

- To order by mail, send check or money order payable to: Elfin Cove Press, 914 Virginia St., Seattle, WA 98101.
- To order by fax, fill out this form and send to (206) 374-2230.
- To order by e-mail, send a credit card order to ECovePress@aol.com.
- To order over the Internet, visit www.elfincovepress.com.

Quantity Discounts: 10–49 copies / less 15%
50 or more copies / less 20%

_____ copies @ $9.95 each   _____

$2.50 shipping and handling (first book)   _____

$1.50 S&H (each additional book)   _____

Washington state residents add 8.6%   _____

Total   _____

MasterCard / Visa (circle one)

Card # _____   _____

Expiration date _____

Signature _____

Ship to (please print):

Name _____

Address _____

City _____ State _____ Zip _____

Telephone number (_____) _____